Dedication

Our thoughts are the driving force behind our actions. But as I have learned thoughts are to be under control and subject to the word of GOD. This book objective is to give you inside from the word of GOD as to how to control and maintain your thoughts under control and in line with the word.

TABLE OF CONTENT

INTRODUCCIÓN

One powerful principle that helps us with managing our thoughts in a more effective way is principal of replacement. The principal I am talking about here involves the power of telling our thoughts that we refuse to be giving into any anxious thoughts. We possess the ability to do this, because as believers we are stronger, we have the greater one living inside. We have the power to resist wanting to have any type of negative thoughts. Exercising authority over what we think is a step in the right direction.

However, if the only step, we take to control the thoughts is confessing with a loud voice we resist having negative thoughts and we stop there; we have not given our minds anything to move towards instead. We must replace the thoughts with new options to think on. The visual behind this principle is if we take a cup of milk and run it under the faucet with water. Even if the cup was entirely full of milk to begin with, as water from the facet starts to fill the cup, the milk gets displaced to the point that only water remains. Begin to fill your mind with the right things and there won't be any room for the negative thoughts to dominate in our thought life.

Chapter 1
Thoughts and
The Word of God

Have you done any spring cleaning lately? How about with your mind? In the same way, you have to routinely root out piles of paper and junk that may be around the house, you also have to be attentive with your thought life and what beliefs you have been allowing to hang around. I once heard my father in the faith Brother Keith Moore say that the Lord had instructed him to evaluate every belief that he had, as to whether it was scriptural or not.

Think about that, evaluate, examine, look in to everything you believe but not just check into it, verify if it is based on the scriptures or if it is just man's idea. I believe there is so much wisdom behind those instruction and is priceless because, if we were dedicated to examining everything we hear in relation to the word, we be able to make sure that what people are saying is either true or not based on the word. This way of living is connected to the amount of success we get to experience in life. Why would it be important to talk about our belief systems and thought life?

Whatever we decide to continually think about is going to impact our believes, which is going to have either a positive or negative outcome in every aspect of our life's, from our feelings, to behaviors, to choices, to even our salvation. If we do not have the right belief system about who Jesus is and what He did for us, we cannot even enjoy a relationship with Him. For the scriptures say in *Romans 10:10, "That if though shalt confess with thy mouth the Lord Jesus, and shalt believe in thine heart that God hath raised him from the dead, though shalt be saved"*.

What we believe and think about continually even impacts the type of person we are and become, *"For as he thinketh in his heart, so is he". Proverbs 23:7.* If we give into thinking that we never be able to amount to anything? That belief will put us on a totally different track in life than the one who believes the words of Jesus in *Mark 9:23* "*If you can believe, all things are possible to Him who believes*". Therefore, it becomes imperative that we take the time to learn how to manage your thought life successfully by using godly principals.

Chapter 2
The Mind-Body Connection

Scientists and Psychologists are now more than ever in agreement about the undeniable power of thoughts and how they can manifest at a physical and emotional level. Many people have been struggling with mental health issues for many years. Some of the issues this people are dealing with is anxiety, depression and because of this mental health issues they are also struggling with physical issues like muscle tension, sleep disorders, and weight problems.

Can you see the connection between those things people constantly think and the way it affects their life? Our thoughts matter! If we think about all the negative things going on in our life, it will impact our body. We could easily lose sleep, get sick, and even lose motivation. But when we are obedient to the scriptures, and think about the right things, we allow health and healing to flow in our life: *A merry [or joyful] heart does good, like medicine, but a broken spirit dries the bones*

Proverbs 17:22. I'm not sure about you, but I want a healthy body, that is why I keep a merry heart! You may be asking yourself Brother Edward is sounds great everything you saying but, how can I manage my thoughts more effectively? We can find in the bible a powerful principal which I truly believe is very helpful if we use it in the process of learning how to manage our thoughts effectively and that is the great principle of replacement.

This principle requires that you open your mouth, that you read your bible, that you pray and that you build a relationship with GOD. This principal will only work if you do your part, because I can't do it for you, and no one else can. You have to say to out loud to yourself, "I do not want to have any more anxious thoughts" or "I don't want to think negatively" Doing this puts us in a place of control and definitely shows that we are acting on one of many ways that are available for us to take steps forward in the right direction.

If all we do is stop at saying something, and don't go pass that stage, go further with reading your bible, praying, and building that relationship with GOD the only thing that will happen is that we be making a bunch of noise and are not giving our mind anything to move towards instead. We must determine in your heart that we will seek the kingdom of GOD first and HIS righteousness, that provides us with the right thing to think on to get rid of negative thoughts and change our belief systems.

The visual behind this principle is if we take a cup of milk and run it under the faucet with water. Even if the cup was entirely full of milk to begin with, as water from the facet starts to fill the cup, the milk gets displaced to the point that only water remains. I am telling you my friend begin to fill your mind with the right things, with the word of GOD and you will never have room for negative thoughts to continue to dominate our thought life. If negative thoughts were to come against you, your heart, your mind and your soul is so full of the word of GOD that you will immediately have the right answer to say like Jesus when the enemy was trying to tempt him "It is writing"

Chapter 3
What will you
think on instead?

In *Philippians 4:8* we can find the answer about what should we be thinking on instead of negative things: *Philippians 4:8 says "Finally, brethren, whatever things are true, whatever things are noble, whatever things are just, whatever things are pure, whatever things are lovely, whatever things are of good report, if there is any virtue and if there is anything praiseworthy meditate on these things"*. This scripture is giving us specific instructions to keep our thoughts clean and clear from any negative thoughts the enemy try to bring our way.

The verse is telling us to be like gatekeepers allowing only authorized thoughts to enter. So, find the scripture that gives you truth, that gives you light about having the right type of thinking and gives you light for more understanding about the way GOD wants us to maintain our minds clear to have peace. As you do this overtime, you train yourself to think like God thinks to the point that when a problem arises, the word just flows out of our mouth to meet the situation.

This will begin to push the things out of your life that do not belong. Don't get discouraged when negative thoughts keep coming back, because I assure you, they will! But as you focus more and more on what GOD has to say about the situation, HIS thoughts and words will start to become bigger on the inside of you than anything else, and this will open the door to God's miracle power to work in your life.

I would like to share something along the lines of our thoughts and how they affect our bodies and feelings that I heard, and it hit me like a bullet to the heart. "Feelings don't hurt you, it's what you do with them that can". You might be thinking "Really? Brother Edward, Feelings don't have to wreak havoc in my life? That's right! You can actually have power over your thoughts and your feelings. If you think about it how else are we supposed to live the abundant life GOD promised in John 10:10 if HE didn't give us the power over our thoughts and feelings.

Let's take a deeper look into what the bible says about the matter. First, we know according to the Word of GOD that **"with GOD all things are possible" Matt 19:26.** So for you to have power over your thoughts and not allowing them to affect your feelings, you first must be in faith that it is possible. A second key in having power over your feelings, is found in *Psalm 23:4 "Yea, though I walk through the valley of the shadow of death, I will fear no evil: for thou art with me; thy rod and thy staff they comfort me." Psalm 23:4*

Now can you imagine walking through the valley of the shadow of death, you're going to have some thoughts raising through your mind during that walk, and feelings are going to start to come up about the current situation you find yourself in. Now those thoughts are going to affect the way you feel,

you may start crying, you may start to feel
happening to your body, sweeting, nervous,
anxious, needs about to give up on you etc.

You might have Goosebumps but if the
word is in your heart, is in your mind, is in
your soul. You be able to keep cool because
you know the verse don't all the sudden stop
in you are walking through the valley of
death, this verse continues and the verse tells
us that we have victory in the middle of it, *I
will fear no evil.*

A second key the scriptures give us about
having power over our thoughts and the
feelings that will accompany those thoughts
which bring with them physical problems is
to remember that we must exercise our will,
as in we must decide to resist the wrong kinds
of thoughts. You may say, but brother
Edward how will I know what thoughts are
wrong? What are the thoughts you saying
that are wrong?

The answer is very simple and is those
constant thoughts that are not in line with the

word and the things we are supposed to think on that were mentioned in *Philippians 4:8 says "Finally, brethren, whatever things are true, whatever things are noble, whatever things are just, whatever things are pure, whatever things are lovely, whatever things are of good report, if there is any virtue and if there is anything praiseworthy meditate on these things"*

As you can see here the are other things that we are supposed to be thinking about and they are also mentioned as part of the fruits of the spirit in *Galatians 5:22, "Love, joy, peace…".* People can run into challenges that are very though, but if all they are doing is resisting to do what GOD says we must do in HIS word we will never be able to stand against the wiles of the enemy.

If your focus is not on doing something about how you need to control your thoughts, you won't be giving your mind an opportunity to change its way of thinking and behaving. Resisting is a good step, but you must also re-set your focus to what you are

trying to move towards. Let's go in the bible
and take a look at a truth that many have read
but have not taken a hold of in their hearts
*Hebrews 12: 2 in the amplified for more insight
into this:* **Therefore then, since we are surrounded
by so great a cloud of witnesses [who have borne
testimony to the Truth], let us strip off and throw
aside every encumbrance (unnecessary weight) and
that sin which so readily (deftly and cleverly)
clings to and entangles us, and let us run with
patient endurance and steady and active
persistence the appointed course of the race that is
set before us, 2 Looking away [from all that will
distract] to Jesus, Who is the Leader and the
Source of our faith.**

The Word of GOD makes sure, to
provide us with clear inside on ways that that
we must act to have transformation in our
way of thinking, our way of acting. The word
shows us that to change, really in an area of
our life, we must look away from whatever it
is we are trying to change, and re-set our
focus onto Jesus, the Word. This is what I
consider a third key in the process of

changing our way of thinking. So whatever feelings might be wreaking havoc in your life, go to the word for the answer, look at it until it becomes real to you on the inside.

That's how we start yielding to the right kinds of feelings and that's how change always takes place, from the inside out. So, if you get angry all the time, read all the scriptures you can on love. If you're sad and depressed, renew your mind with scriptures on the joy and peace of God.

As you do this overtime, the godly seed you have put in your heart will start to come out of your mouth. *"For out of the abundance of the heart his mouth speaks" (Luke 6:45).* And your mouth holds another powerful key that we will talk about as it relates to power over your thoughts. *"And if anyone does not offend in speech [never says the wrong things], he is a fully developed character and a perfect man, able to control his whole body and to curb his entire nature. James 3:2* AMP Catch that last part of the scripture. *"to curb his entire nature"* What do you think is the main thing that makes the connection to this way of thinking?

The answer is what we say. God makes it very clear in the scriptures that your tongue is linked to having the power that we need over our body, including our thoughts. Often you probably have heard people and maybe you say, "I feel so achy and tired" or "Well, I'm such and such ethnicity, and it's in my blood to have a short fuse." Well those words started as a thought, and then you gave them power to become a feeling for you that was dealing with any situation and let me ask you, what happened after that?

You did exactly what the enemy wanted you to do, you open your big mouth and said a bunch of negative things and confession over your body, over you attitude, over your health and even say the same things to other people. Can you see this? there is so much power in your tongue but the power that is given to the tongue comes from your thoughts.

If you continue saying and declaring these kinds of things, you will have exactly what you say! Because the thought that was in your mind, dropped to your heart, you believe it and so you spoke it, for the good or for the bad. Do yourself a favor and start asking the Lord to point out the areas where you might need to make some adjustments when it comes to the things you are saying.

Make an honest quality decision for yourself today as you are reading this book that you will seek GOD to show you in HIS word ways that you can use to start renewing your mind to have better control over your thoughts. When talking about our thoughts and how they are supposed to be connected to the Word of God, we are talking about how what we think on continually makes a big impact on what we believe, which impacts how we feel, behave, and the choices we make.

The choices we make determine the course and direction of our life. When we

THOUGHTS HAVE NO CONTROL OVER YOUR MOUTH

THOUGHTS HAVE NO CONTROL OVER YOUR MOUTH

Edward G. Valdez

choose to think on what God's Word says, we train ourselves to think like God thinks to the point that when a problem arises, the word just flows out of our mouth to meet the situation.

Chapter 4
Awareness is Key

If we are not aware of the maneuvers of the enemy *(2 Corinthians 2:11)*, how can we have a victorious life? Is impossible for us to be victorious without the knowledge about the word of GOD and without hearing the word we won't faith to stand against the enemy. Faith comes by hearing and one of the most effective strategies the enemy uses against us is thoughts and suggestions that go against the Word of God.

We see it in the Garden of Eden when Satan tried to twist the words of God when he spoke to Eve *(Genesis 3:1-5)*. I have come to realize that with many Christians that I have spoken with over the years, it's easy for us to lose awareness of what we are doing. When habits whether positive or negative are stablished deep in our way of life we end up doing them automatically and if you think about it even without giving much conscious thought.

You can see this in the simple example of when you have traveled to work or some other place and then realized you did not quite remember every turn or light you took to get to your destination. Similarly, it's easy to lose track of what you are thinking on throughout the day. But for real change to take place in your life, you must be aware of what we are thinking and doing, so we can monitor whether we are on the right track.

Let's take a few moments to do a quick self-check to see how you are doing in managing your thought life. How much of your cares are you casting onto the Lord? (*1 Peter 5:7*). It's easy to read scriptures like *1 Peter 5:7* that seemingly "encourage" us to do things like cast our cares on the Lord and think "oh, yeah, that's good". But are you doing this?

It may be that when you think about it, or you hear a message reminding you to do this, you do this for some time. However, it's what we continue in that produces results in our lives *(John 8:31-32KJV)*. If you find that you cast your care but are taking the care back, seek God and ask for wisdom about how you might break the cycle.

He might show you to start acting in a certain area or to feed more on certain scriptures in the Word of God to resist fears that you are allowing to persist in your life. When are you most vulnerable to wrong kinds of thoughts and feelings throughout the day? There are times when we are all more vulnerable to wrong kinds of thoughts and feelings.

If you're late to work, or you happened to have a challenging day with clients, haven't eaten in several hours, you're more susceptible to giving place to certain kinds of thoughts and feelings, those feelings could be perhaps anger or frustration. Start locating specific moment that you may be more likely to yield to wrong thoughts and feelings and check in with the Holy Spirit for direction.

The Lord will equip you with knowledge about things you might do to avoid problem scenarios and resolve difficulties that arise. Sometimes we might think big adjustments are needed for progress to happen in our lives. This may be true in some cases however in some other cases it may only take small adjustments. The enemy knows that he can't win against the word of God. However, in *1 Peter 5:8 it says, "The devil walks about like a roaring lion, seeking whom he may devour"*.

Who can he devour? Anyone who consistently yields to wrong kinds of thoughts and feelings. If as believers, we are not submitting to the Word of God and are yielding to wrong thoughts, he can achieve his goal of stealing, killing, and destroying in our lives (John 10:10). Let's stay more on track and be mindful to be on guard for moments when we may be more susceptible to wrong kinds of thoughts.

There are many ways for us to locate indicators of progress as we set any goals that we are looking to attain. A big part in been able to utilize those indicators in future situations is maintaining an awareness of our progress this is critical in moving forward. For example, let's say you are in the move to lose weight, a scale can help you maintain an awareness about your weight if is going up or down.

The way you look as time passes can also give you an indication about your physical appearance for how well you are doing. When it comes to renewing your mind, it may seem somewhat more challenging to remain aware of your thoughts consistently since they are less tangible. However, remember that we have talked about how our thoughts can impact every area of our life's and what you continually think about will manifest in ways that are easy to detect.

For instance, when a person yields to anger, how could we detect it? Think about yourself, how do you react? Their body language, facial expressions, as well as verbal language are cues to what they have been thinking about. Likewise, start paying more attention to these indicators regularly yourself to see how well you are doing. If your facial expressions make it so that others seeing you want to be as far away from you as possible, you may not be entirely casting your cares onto the Lord.

Remember that to control our thoughts is not just a nice thing to do it is a Command not an Encouragement It's the doers that get results in life. Verses like *1 Peter 5:7* are not an encouragement they are a command. Just as so many other scriptures where Jesus said, **"Let not your heart be troubled" (John 14:1; 14:27).** Make it a habit to cast your care (without taking it back), trust God, and seek God for wisdom. Maintain awareness of when your thoughts are going in the wrong direction so you can quickly make **an** adjustment.

I am reminded of a Word that the Lord shared with Gloria Copeland years ago, *"In consistency lies the key"*. When we consistently take thoughts from the enemy, we get the results he wants us to have. However, when we consistently take thoughts from what GOD has to say, we get HIS results. Results that will take us higher and higher into His plan and purpose for our lives. Amen!

And we also thank God continually for this, that when you received the word of God [concerning salvation] which you heard from us, you welcomed it not as the word of [mere] men, but as it truly is, the word of God, which is effectually at work in you who believe [exercising its inherent, supernatural power in those of faith]. 1 Thessalonians 2:13 (AMP)

ABOUT THE AUTHOR

Edward Valdez is the founder of EGVIM. He is a man according to the heart of God, ready and willing to do what the Lord tells him to do. His military experience has given him a soldier mentality that makes it easy to be used by the Lord, since he is always ready to receive orders from the head of the church. In response to the Lord's direction, Edward and his wife Jade moved with their two children to Sarasota Florida.

There is no doubt that God has abundantly blessed Edward through the anointed teachings and training they receive from their spiritual parents Keith and Phyllis Moore. Edward is a living witnesses of God's healing power, provision and blessing in his live. Brother Edward positively impacts everyone who crosses his path.

GOD has specifically put in his heart to reach the Hispanic population. His heart is that all learn to be led by the Spirit, grow in a superior faith and abundant love. He believes that if Latin America obtains the Truth about God's love, the power of forgiveness and how to walk in His perfect will, they will experience a movement of God as they have never done before!

THE TRUTH, THE WORD OF

GOD ALWAYS DISCOVERS,

DISSIPATE THE INCREDULITY AND

LIES OF THE ENEMY.